Color & Light

COLOR & LIGHT

Kyle Schlesinger

Dusie 2021

Layout and design by DUSIE
www.dusie.org | Block Island

Some of these poems have appeared in *Blazing Stadium*, *Fell Swoop*, & *Hurricane Review*. Special thanks to Lithic Press & Bookstore for generously hosting a residency in Fruita, Colorado, where many of these poems were written or revised by the Book Cliffs.

Cover by Nate Ethier. *Skipper*, 2019, 44 x 66 inches.
ISBN-13: 978-1-944253-09-7
LCCN: 2020952183

for Alasdair —
who makes everything more interesting

CONTENTS

I am a human being. Nothing that is human is foreign to me.

— Terrence Afar

Attention is the purest form of prayer.

— Simone Weil

Everything resurfaces.

— Tom Raworth

Color & Light

FACE

for Jim

Let me show you
How to draw a
Human face

Crushed charcoal
Oil markers
Ink jabs
Splatters

Ground down
With a fist pressed
Hard into sawdust

Then the glue then
From total chaos
A vivid self-portrait
The living daylight

Life begins with abstraction
Form is found through
Experience

That's how you draw a face

TRUANT

Spry sunset orange flakes
Out of my tree a casket
So called converge risk
Thunderbolt converse
With the unlimited if
Playbook offhand nots
Failed to mention lots
Repeat my situation add
To the atones and repeat
On delete casual brain
Said nuff afternoon said

In bins history growths
Walk receptions hanker
To the elevens makeover
Past flowers on trees
Knees bend I do too
I do that bus driver
Bored as bombshell
Misfits shake hands take
Found wallets and do ring
The whole christian thing
I get it and make way

One light down winter larks
An afternoon to franchise
Cells coagulate and so on
Roses luminescent where's
Where there is no crosswalk there
Repeat after me street talking
Mime's chainsaw have ceased
And the clearing is clear for a spell
Evening everyone evacuates
To their own rooms setting up
Studios where cribs used to elevate

Putting in new floors and faucets
Between actual doors and rayon
As curfew scold centerfold
At the store I've been making living
One hundred times or more and
The obvious moron is over it
Caters to contraband in hallways
Brownie in pink clothes implodes
Too rancid to mention gestation
Cut it short like history
Angle of repose

WE ALSO SELL FISH

Stepping out never drove
In a car being called alive
Precepts of chance
Stepping out never drove
When the time comes
Be called you'll see
Precepts of chance
Be seen around
Stepping out be called

THE ULTIMATE JAMS

with Paul Maziar & James Yeary

The ultimate jams
Beneath a bed of crayons
My heart on a string

You recite fables
I fold like a chair
You're out there

Brittle kale crumbles
Dr. Pepper gots guzzled
Moontower pizza

Where's your cousin at
The one with the underbite
That's what I'm thinking

They say, 'do the math'
Stop at the Firkin Tavern
A name to go by

A-1 Food Market
Orion weeps in his dreams
Moon over subway

The key of water
Nothing to do with balance
Just sing normally

That saucy fucker
Breaking some bread with Suzy
The Body of Christ

Winona Ryder
Professionally known as
Winona Ryder

Meet Gary Snyder
Born May 8, 1930
A man of letters

Do part d'you
Beat that poem
part, depart too

His hair was like bread
A whole entire loaf of it
The wind a weakling

But who can I trust
Hall sound familiar on nose
Whoever it is

Someone I can trust
Hall sound like the former on
Whoever come back

Flame out fame window
Scrub in reverse osmosis
This mixtape's for you

Freak out and fall back
Look it up you'll see yourself
I don't mean that

BLUE PLATE SPECIAL

for Neeli

Pull out the stars
And replace them
With a pristine
Blue butt plug

What is there
To say
Runs through
My mind
Citronella tin

Wooden bowl
Who you were
When they
Were them

Local objects
What was it like
Clouds' edges
Shimmer obscured
By smoke

Description
Illuminates
A cold fireplace
Pink tiles

Somewhere between
Soft rock
We look up
Fault as if it were
A bottle rocket

Exploding in
The basement
As if nobody
Had done that

Before
Transposed by
Light and its
Absence red
Penetrating black

Book Cliffs
Why not
Order a sandwich
For the morning

Pealing out
In your dreams
Framing pictures
My hands
Are a little wet

But clean
Thrashing the
Chandelier
With a crutch

Split a spliff with
The new neighbor
Skylight falls
Eyes like Buber

YOUR NAME HERE

And I woke up over Colorado
Thinking of you, white wine
Ritz crackers, two kinds of lifetimes
I'm off on another Sam Shepard kick

I'd do it all again, why I don't know
All the way to the Hocking Hills
Snowcapped peaks blistering shoulders
Hair shorter than I remember

That faded tie dye in the closet
And cold, cold nights I'd walk
A country mile with you in peace
Kicking up the cold, cold country

The Gay Hamlet

Is a nice place to visit

PAPER RAIN

for Lorraine

Time is where
You put it
Me as a shape

Which side
Is your good side
Physical graffiti

Grotto at night
Indifferent to
Crusades

Blurring oblivion
Microscope hits
Sunset on dash

Case the green
Fade into night
Remain to be seen

COLOR & LIGHT

for Danny

There is a natural history of life
A point on the pinwheel that
Is easy to parse in place but
What is the word for the shade
Of snowberry on the way to the
Library when the stars are so bright
The flowering leaves leave you tonight

Electric noise shooting offshore
Running through finger paint
Orange dashes between
Peppered Indian paintbrush
Yellowing slowing down time
Eight days from now sprinklers
Blow in the wind and rain

As you reach for the sky
As you peach for the cold
As the hummingbirds skyrocket
Yellow ball corner pocket
As the blue world revolves
Mention the good times
Hovering on the run

Resembles a thistle the shape
Of the sound of mauve aloud
Slurring shades vibrate
How heavy the light feels
On the eyelids of midnight
Faded by heat beat down by day
When it came to in the dry grass

Wide awake and sputtering
I shall forge the blade of my own
Substance and it may not be a blade
Goodnight Molly as the walls
Fell away through the shadows
Where things were as they are
Standing waves in either canyon

Soaking up utopia
Rocks twist from trees
Sway with the west wind
As the darkness putters around
A stranger putting their jeans on
Passages fly from the moving window
Tumbling in the blue dirt of paradise

Making your own days
Sun moves through shade
As shade moves through shadows

And shadows fade a jitterbug
Nightlight flickers through days
Alone among the cows the
Clouds dream of new weather

NO TRESPASSING

No trespassing
Reads the sign
Outside the Kingdom
Hall of Jehovah's Witnesses

Three vultures on the streetlamp
Next day a man with a rifle
Was escorted from the Kingdom
That's religion for 'ya

I'M WRITING A POEM HERE

When the streets are slick
And leaves heavy with sunshine
I feel so light I could whisper

All secret histories to please the breeze
But the wind blew my daughter away
Leaving only a shadow in sand

The room was room temperature
It was as dark as Tuesday
When a taxi rolled up to my feet

And the glass perspired
A brick in a trash can
Rolling down the hill

So we hop in and roll
A tree-lined highway hopped up on
Espresso and grand old Victorians

Edges

EDGES

The city sleeps in on
Right angles late into sun
Ordinary afternoon's white
Taillight autumn denim
Just then marathon street
Flows into a bank of gravel
The usual assassins stand
Up for fingering and explode

The Greek came over
For a better look
At the spiral windsock
Flickering in Topeka
Or Narragansett or
Ayahuasca shadowing the mesa
The sidewalk says who's swelling
Like healthy veins in a hurricane

Be that as it may
The bunker is perpendicular to
The hammock to the
Letter the brow beaten
Meridian yellow on a cliff

Mendocino mysterious
Seven-foot butler with hairline
Recedes into waves

Billowing afternoon
Light autumn denim
Crisp as frost on the window
Where the crest
Melts down your back
Sand into glass dreams
Mulberry rolls grass to sleep
At your feet for the faint of sheep

When the night says yes
But goes on too long
Gown candles glow
Around the shadows gold
Waiting for one more
Short story by Lucia Berlin
Levitation is the only thing
I care about anymore

I look at myself in the mirror
As if it's morning
Fingering lipstick and
Watching the steam
Come off the waterfall

On a January morning in
Vermont and it's 1983
Just Patti and me

WHAT IT ALL MEANS

It's vaguely hypnotic
So people probably
Shouldn't do it

CONFESSIONAL HAIKU

I oft prefer the
Sentimental ZZ Top
Afterburner years

Over the acclaimed
Shredding riffs that critics claim
Established the band

As a major force
In rock and roll history
But that is just me

THE END OF NOT DATING

The era of not-dating has come to an end & if I ever choose not to not-date someone again, and should we choose to not not-not date again, I hope it's as nice as not-not-dating someone not quite like you.

THE GOOD LIFE

for Joanne

All of this every day
Everyone dying
And every day just seems less familiar
Every this and that
And I wonder where you are
Counting on my hands
But hands are just shapes
A hometown I'll never go back to
It's been a hell of a year
That much I can tell you
Small changes and poems pass
Some stick and I'm sick of
Being sick of loss and losing
The only loss I've ever known
And imagined I'd be where you
Are now if I had a tendency
Toward self-pity and wonder
Why I'm alone and if you are too
On a beach I can only imagine
Lascivious and loquacious
And still at rest
And in the morning I heard
A water bird over the Cape

What kind I do not know
Then it occurred to me
That water birds don't sound
Like any other kind of bird
Places to go

FOUND POEM

Fave movie: Horror
Fave book: Classical
Fave means: Nihilist
Fave philosopher: Bertrand Russell

POEM

And they were young again
When snow had fallen
Off the curb

Horses on the roof
Like the lobster there
Heart of hearts

No need for all
Out of town
Saw them

In a magazine
Had a feeling
That's beautiful

Behind our backs
Freedom of a people
Crowd drifted by

Closer to the camera
Never talked to strangers
Playing a bad hand

THE ODDS

On the tarmac, I have the feeling I could die at any time. That's always true, but there's something about sitting still on the runway, eyes closed, waiting to fly. That quiet moment between two worlds. I'm inclined to ruminate on the ups and downs. A lot of people do, and for a moment the airplane is like a little church where some people feel bored, some impatient, some completely themselves, some somewhere else entirely or ecstatically. But that's just everyday life on the tarmac. It occurs to me that I'm almost forty years old and I've never served in a war, not even drafted, not even basic training. How many people my age can say that? And I don't just mean Americans, and I don't even mean just the twentieth century. I mean everywhere, always, the fact of war and mortality. What are the odds? Never broke a bone. Never had a prescription drug. Never had an operation. Never been in a car wreck. Never been deported, never been arrested. Sure, a lot of this has to do with class and race and gender. A lot of people have died. Why do people have to die? A few months ago, I wasn't so sure that death was real. But I'm getting convinced. Slow on the uptake. I've never been killed, stabbed, beaten, or shot, and I haven't killed, stabbed, beaten, or shot anyone. Point being. Sometimes these thoughts on the runway get at where I'm at, and that's a lucky place to be, I guess, on the outskirts of somewhere, going to the outskirts of somewhere else, expecting to fly.

Then Again

THEN AGAIN

It’s not the spirit
It’s the letter

•

Embers become flames
Flames become embers
Between you me and

•

Bees are suffering
Sit with the itch

•

Chase to the cut
Let’s talk medieval
How come we now

•

I'll say differently
I won't say literally

•

Stirring compost
Living slower
Scattered

•

My history
Is paisley

•

Curtain ties
Wildflowers
Karen

•

The tide goes in
And out again

•

There's no time
To do anything
But be alive

•

The sky
Vibrates

•

This is somewhere
We could be
Sensible vampires

•

Dogs come
And go

•

The only thing
That interests me
Is transformation

•

Dirt roads
Signs

•

Charisma
Is the cult
Of insecurity

•

DMT
Bores me

•

The prettiest
Florist
In town

•

Which way
Is the stüpa?

•

A pest
Can only
Destroy itself

•

Turn around
In the shade

•

Soda
Love
Bubbles

•

Eschew
Obfuscation

•

Listening to d.a. levy
At Smithson's jetty

•

for Fritz

Rain
Clouds
Hail
Tears
Sunshine

•

Reading Zinn
At the Pelican Inn

•

Bill's
Transcendental
Side

•

Taboos
On the move

•

Looks like
I'm the last man
Camping

•

Picking up
Speed

•

Or just
Smoking dope
In a van

•

Zeitgeist
Hyphenate

•

Just me
And the fuzz
On the green

•

Cat by the door
Looking for more

•

Some people
You just can't
Reach

•

Verdant notebook
Red Mountain Pass

•

Avalanche
Aspens
Swell

•

Amused
By the news

•

If Ruscha
Knew what I knew
We'd have the same IQ

•

Dicey
Weekend

•

Nerves
Then the sensation
Of nerves

•

The nerves
Splurge

•

As one hand
Jiggles the handle

•

The other draws
Concentric
Eels

•

Seldom
Random

•

Toy blonde
In sunglasses
The sand

•

Leaves
In puddles
•

Sledding
In paradise

•

Over the
Handlebars

•

New friends

•

Their smiles
Rain on

•

The most bucolic
Mailman yet

•

Cone
Flowers

•

Think with
Your eyes

•

What were Lew Welch's
Last words?

•

Parachute

•

There is
Parking lots

•

In my hair
I'm coming through

•

Cubbyholes

•

Morning
Minimalism

•

Sharkskin

•

Some people
Just disappear

Far & Away

Far & Away

out of town found yesterday
what else expect the beautiful
forget whole thing do at dawn

meanwhile tropics go to work
with money hand happens next
then somebody not clear who

memo to self okay it's Laos
better get over the body
thank you no what else expect

before you ask something's come up
evening's long gone one light on
tide rolls in and out again

milky reeds back behind wheel
made in Singapore it's stars
palm beneath fender come in

make yourself at home sugar's sugar
last place left first before you ask
answer me this who saw once

seated bathrobe up stairs dash
no way to refuse your breathing
it's okay it's breathing still grasping

it's stars I could see maybe
something like that highlight on wall
please continue from a jar

there are a natural progression in life
why not that of true sepia
neither had spoken crest of light

for thought of my being
that Monday to be annuity
I could see maybe bends darts

pure recall anyone ever said
anything about want only in dreams
talk arm off stoop face except

then there's music neither had spoken
eyes of green far be it from me
even about the likes of such

fuck you money idea of form
coffee kills time no exceptions
word got out cut to close-up

drip on the run solution a vein
permissions afford a bad idea
study ceiling eyes of green

the routine gets to know you
as if that weren't enough consider
Maryland last to arrive

side by side on an empty stomach
cut to close-up living room faces
smoke gets in your eyes

mind of clone windows face south
reason of doubt season of which
can you imagine a pencil so yellow

flick of the switch garage door
opens wide be one with chalk
hands lay palm up in lap

living room faces eyes close mouth
may appear empty do you read
tropical tan on the park asphalt

reach for the wall all my faults
armchairs each flick of the switch
why so late with own table

oh it's only you line is a hinge
peanut variety heard this one before
the cappuccino came dead or dying

hue of shadow clouded over
American express called by name
reason hits the road do come again

you know who why so late
of human intelligence as blank is to
just how much does silence cost

work the lobby tell me this
please think before end in sight
clouded over the ultimate makeover

seventy-four having second thoughts
down to the lobby pay phone rain
show me something I can't inhale

dance makes wet drawers twin
neon periods g'bye inside out
three stories too small triangle north

where the big glass door shun where
the ultimate makeover you shunt
cohere over here near the elevator

primary color me pink half the cops
all the actors bank of pay telephones
four six five neon periods g'bye

on snow days took horse tranquilizers
nine one nine one across bone
white bristles a certain somebody

pale white inertia still deep in the sauce
that's Hollywood remind me to tell you
all things we did crazy story

inert but alert trouble tightens the belt
teen story on snow days took
terry cloth hotel let's hear it state capitals

dead actors don't want to know
a funhouse mirror into jacking
will never be the same weather fit tight

remind me to tell you into flames
real live DJ drifts away
about the weather about the salad

country's glass major money
dated it ever have something going
twenty four or twenty five a little too

a little too fell in with what
used to be called the wrong crowd
into flames real live DJ

the duck's good tonight why
you tell me where will it end
just routine sunshine in the small hours

there's something twenty four
or inside me be seen in
the neighborhood what happened

liberty's knocking buzz off
right to left privacy to be
no longer think I'll go home

you bet inside the lobby
garage around through a glass door
think about it four of them

be seen in traded information
all rights to the soundtrack
still unfound back over

everything poking at this recourse
think I'll go home in pieces
speculate about just remembered

most of them short and simple
keep it brief in a one-room studio
no need on the top floor

this was the late fifties the late
late fifties and running
who wants that then what

next time use speculate about
sunshine smile on tiptoe
wore the pants coupe wide open

rifling glove as you well know
one and the same this was the late
never defect back to the wall

at the far end a gloomy bay
books in the black it all began on
whose thousand-yard stares

until that day when the last
variegated cloud lifts off the roof
and it was here on the radio

in what was always a beverage
back to the wall while waiting tables
never been any waiting since

names drop nobody hears
mortar and brick when the light is like
when the last question repeats itself

your story here never the same
ballpoint looks good in pictures
daydream on mute no limit

turnstiles into wishes why bother
be curious torches fire in movies
that's how it goes on a bicycle

with radio on the same old song
and you disappear your story here
from the book and suddenly

unconditional you something like allegory
sun's rays into old gold jigsaw
slabs of black slate be curious

chinks of light just beyond crest
top of drive country blacktop
by tall pines whose branches

were bowed under their burdens
of snow and ice no need to know
forget about being on the mouth

a dog's a dog but lacking finesse
hang the cost on a clear conscience
slots to pay off some political doubts

anyway it seems whole world smiles
before chop landed story never ran
catch ghost before dying

no need to know iced vodka
without turning in a Wendy's
when that happens phone doodles

I want you glasses take off
look at that watch who needs it
twilight snowman spun out

never said life follows
dubious glance as if
a word with you sure

dirty money sip coffee
continue reading upside down
lower lip frowned as if

think of ears twilight snowman
medium hard return with drinks
show me a sign no longer new

as you were back on the line
pleasure from pleasure by the time
on the shore of an artificial lake

cul-de-sac ends you were saying
depending on traffic blue-green
order by phone during bouts

return with drinks place an event
coasting down slopes your dreams
d'you have in mind a vermouth

it's nine thirty-three headlights off
an artificial lake gets the collar
where riot girls go to retire

commercial laundry only a nod
glossy toes snow globe
right foot on curb

shake off cold nobody answer
but why come here see the subject
who was color matter of fact

know how it is where riot girls go
sunshine don't owe a dime
then maybe into snowy night

eye moves behind tinted glass
blue with money shake off cold
do me a favor weren't there

somewhere west of Cheyenne
the snow failed to cease
divided by a nose yeah the horse

in the big chair they neigh
clasp hands recall everything
when a commercial came on

this haircut's killing not bad
recall everything of course
wasn't there for what were after

elbows on knees loaded question
watching the snow fall upon night
they neigh fingers into glass

hang on phone seen and heard
didn't see rose the horse
forehead below a shock of yellow

a point slid to a halt
like I was saying in a wingback
a shuttle blows up

try for twin beds remove glass ceiling
recall what's been said hang on phone
adore the real voice bar lights aim

blue neon vacancy warning flares
whose names needn't be mentioned
in other words like I was saying

threat was grave cinematic amnesia
plot of land headlights at wreck
nothing personal fact is

do the numbers thickets for eyebrows
summered number think tanks
ship through the door talking blizzard

with two *b*'s and two *t*'s enjoy it
butts go stale outer ends of
cinematic amnesia dark resign

or is it spit *and* image got urge
women's shoes other than magazines
little of interest summered number

think tanks almost next door
diddles don't know coming to boil
on electric stove a vending machine

on-again off-again bay gelding
double-park cancel your dream
talking to the floor all night

I'm just sayin' Chinese red
when it comes down to it
alter fiasco women's shoes

other conditions may apply
alien outline never by name
was empty cot on oval rag rug

turn up heat talking to the floor
thought everyone nailed the guy
knew a way in antics its been

homegrown money heady times
in and of itself by any means
what began must've when

about then nothing but letter
sure hit the spot of course eternity
native tongue on the run

nailed the guy don't mean business
young people today new fad
atmosphere maybe even ambiance

changing the subject would cost less
must've when but still too much
about what that's what 'ah' means

pigeonholes reach into
hoping to find is a true copy
much interested in mementos

distance from distance there isn't one
take the question as silenced
skin pants lazy fair

like I told you about what
up to the farm and look around
never did understand black bag it

dollar for dollar call and rise
only this afternoon distance from distance
that was this afternoon walk away from

and the time after that was covered in
slow motion shot down the hatch
diplomacy's maiden name imagine

Praise for Color & Light

Stealthy, low-key hilarious & perfectly observed observations of lived American life containing the strewn remnants of several decades of personal & cultural detritus. Slow-rolled perambulations that gather some strange sort of wise anti-wisdom, & constantly perched at the intersection where one genre of song morphs into another. In this particular instance let's say.... Honky Tonk to Cosmic American Country.

— Michael Klausman

A smart collection of poems representing the panoramic range of Kyle Schlesinger's talents. 'Far & Away,' a brilliant rigorous formal experiment in language, is the culminating work among more casual and sometimes cinematic poems. A real page-turner with unpredictable joys along the way.

— Annabel Lee

Objects don't have color (they give off light) and words don't *have* meaning (they give off vibration). Color and meaning are ours to determine and agree upon, but what if, first, we sift through our colloquial phrases, our idiomatic expressions, our perceptual experiences, until we enter a world of mutuality rather than human centrality? A poet of both Exteroception and Interoception at once, Kyle Schlesinger asks his reader to 'Think with / Your Eyes,' 'Eyes like Buber.' At turns both funny and heartbreaking, *Color & Light* reminds us that meaning is not intrinsic; it is relational—'I'll say differently / I won't say literally.'

— Sasha Steensen

photograph by Alan Bernheimer

Kyle Schlesinger is a poet, printer, and professor. Recent books include *A New Kind of Country* (Chax Press, 2020), *None of Us*, a collaboration with Ted Greenwald (Kin Press, 2020), *A Poetics of the Press* (Ugly Duckling, 2021). He resides in Austin, where he serves as the proprietor of Cuneiform Press.

SIE
DU

www.ingramcontent.com/pod-product-compliance
Ingram Content Group UK Ltd.
Pitfield, Milton Keynes, MK11 3LW, UK
UKHW041842200726
13854UKWH00005BA/1890
9 781944 253097